CW01522277

The Walking Reset

*Simple Steps to Boost Mood, Imp
Daily Habit That Lasts*

By Amelia Walsh

Foreword

Welcome — and thank you for picking up *The Walking Reset*.

This book is part of the *Everyday Reset* series, a collection of gentle, practical guides to help you reset your habits and reconnect with what matters most. In a world that often pushes for extremes — do more, go faster, be better — these books offer something quieter, yet deeply powerful: a return to simple, sustainable choices that support your wellbeing.

Each title in the series focuses on one small area of life — like decluttering your space, cultivating gratitude, or, as you'll find here, building a steady walking habit. These are not quick fixes or rigid routines. They are invitations. Small shifts. Everyday resets.

I wrote *The Walking Reset* because walking changed my life in ways I didn't expect. It grounded me when I felt scattered. It gave me space when my mind was full. And it reminded me that movement doesn't have to be intense to be transformative.

My hope is that this book will do the same for you — not through pressure or perfection, but through encouragement, self-kindness, and the quiet strength of showing up one step at a time.

Wherever you are right now, this is a fresh start.

Let's begin — gently.

With warmth,
Amelia Walsh

Also in the *Everyday Reset* series:

- o *The Decluttering Reset*
- o *The Gratitude Reset*
- o *The Habit Reset*
- o *The Connection Reset*

CONTENTS

Introduction: A Gentle Reset, One Step at a Time 2

Chapter One: Why Walking is the Ultimate Daily Reset 6

Chapter Two: Resetting Your Routine: How to Start and Keep Going 12

Chapter Three: The Mind-Body Reset: Calm, Clarity, and Confidence 19

Chapter Four: Making Your Walk a Daily Joy 26

Chapter Five: Tracking Your Reset — Without Pressure or Perfection 33

Chapter Six: Walking Through Real Life: Resetting in Hard Moments 41

Chapter Seven: Real Resets: Walking Stories from Everyday Lives 50

Chapter Eight: The 30-Day Walking Reset Challenge 57

Final Reflections: Walking as a Lifelong Reset 65

Introduction: A Gentle Reset, One Step at a Time

Not so long ago, I was feeling stuck — not in any dramatic, life-falling-apart way, but in that quiet, everyday sort of way many of us experience. I was tired, uninspired, and restless. My energy was low, my mood was unpredictable, and the idea of starting a "proper" fitness routine felt exhausting before I even began.

I wasn't looking for a miracle. I just wanted to feel better — more grounded, more awake, more like me.

And so, almost without thinking, I went for a walk.

It wasn't a power walk, or part of a challenge, or tracked with an app. I simply put on my trainers, stepped outside, and started moving. The air was cool, the sky was overcast, and the walk was short. But I came back feeling noticeably different: my head clearer, my shoulders lower, my heart lighter.

So, I did it again the next day. And the day after that. One walk at a time, I began to feel like myself again.

This walking journey was my own small reset — a simple shift that helped me feel like myself again.

The Habit We Overlook

When we think of improving our health, we often think big: join a gym, start a diet, sign up for something that requires gear, schedules, or sweat. We think if it doesn't hurt, it doesn't count. But the truth is, most of us don't need big changes — we need consistent, manageable actions that feel good enough to stick with.

Walking is one of the most underrated forms of movement there is. It's free. It's accessible. It's gentle on the body but powerful in its effects. And when done daily, it creates a foundation for physical and mental wellbeing that few other habits can match.

Yet because it's so simple, many people dismiss it.

We tell ourselves it's "not enough." That it won't lead to real results. That it's not worth scheduling into our already full lives.

But let me tell you this: walking regularly — even for 20 minutes a day — can improve your cardiovascular health, lift your mood, help you sleep better, support healthy weight management, and clear the mental clutter that builds up with everyday stress.

It's not flashy. It's not trendy. But it works.

This Book is for You If...

- You're tired of complicated fitness routines that don't stick

- You want to feel better physically and emotionally without overhauling your life

- You've lost motivation and need a fresh, realistic start

- You don't consider yourself "sporty" or "fit" but want to move more

- You're busy, overwhelmed, or burnt out

- You want a simple habit that fits into your real life, not the life you wish you had

- Greater emotional resilience
- Better self-esteem and outlook

For many people, walking becomes a form of moving meditation. The rhythm of your steps, the fresh air, the quiet focus — all of it contributes to a calmer mind and lighter mood. It's why many people who walk regularly describe it not just as exercise, but as a form of therapy.

If you're looking for a **walking exercise for mental wellness**, this habit could be a game-changer.

You Don't Have to Walk for Hours

One of the most common misconceptions about walking is that it has to be long, fast, or complicated to be effective. In reality, **small, consistent efforts beat occasional big ones every time**.

A 15–30 minute walk each day is a powerful foundation. It adds up over time in ways that are both visible and invisible.

This book is about creating a **walking habit for health and energy**, not about walking marathons (though you might surprise yourself one day!). What matters most is consistency — showing up for yourself in small ways, even when you're tired, busy, or don't feel like it.

And the beauty of walking is that it can be built into everyday life. You don't need to "make time" as much as you need to see walking as a natural part of your routine. It can be:

- A walk to the shops instead of driving
- A lunchtime loop around the office park

- A stroll after dinner with a partner, dog, or podcast
- A short walk before your morning coffee
- Even pacing around your garden while on a call

Every step counts.

Why Walking Helps With Weight Loss (and Why That's Not the Only Goal)

Many people are drawn to walking to support their physical health — especially weight management or fat loss. And rightly so.

A regular walking routine helps burn calories, improves metabolism, and reduces abdominal fat when combined with a sensible eating pattern. But beyond the physical, walking also helps reduce emotional and stress-related eating, and supports better sleep — both of which are crucial to long-term weight balance.

If you've searched for a **simple walking plan for fat loss** or wondered whether you can **lose weight walking every day**, the answer is yes — provided you stay consistent and pair it with supportive lifestyle habits.

But it's worth saying this, too: **walking offers so much more than what the scale shows.** It improves how you feel, how you think, how you sleep, and how you show up in your life. Weight loss may be a goal — and that's valid — but don't miss the deeper gains along the way.

The Emotional Benefit of Moving Forward

One of the most powerful things about walking is what it symbolises: movement, direction, momentum.

On days when you feel emotionally stuck or mentally scattered, walking offers a way forward — physically and metaphorically. Each step becomes a small act of agency. You are moving, even if just around the block. You are breathing. You are participating in your own wellbeing.

Walking gives you space — literally and mentally. Space to process thoughts, shift your mood, or simply escape the noise of modern life. For many people, a regular walk becomes a sacred pause in the day — a chance to reset, reflect, and return with greater clarity.

If you're overwhelmed by all the things you "should" be doing to improve your health, let this be a starting point. Let walking be enough, for now.

You Don't Need to Be Fit to Start

One of the best things about walking is that it doesn't require you to be fit before you begin. In fact, walking helps build that fitness — gently, gradually, and sustainably.

This is the ideal **daily fitness routine for beginners**, especially if you've felt intimidated by gyms, injured by high-impact exercise, or simply lost in a world of fitness influencers and 12-week challenges.

Walking meets you where you are. You can start slow. You can walk in short bursts. You can rest and try again tomorrow.

And because it's low-impact, walking supports your **joint health, balance, and flexibility**, especially as we get older — making it perfect for adults over 40, 50, or beyond.

A Habit That Changes With You

The best habits are the ones that evolve with your life — not against it. Walking is flexible. It can be quiet or social. Fast or gentle. Urban or rural. Short or long. Morning, noon, or night.

It doesn't require you to change who you are. It simply invites you to show up — again and again — with a bit of curiosity and kindness.

Over time, what begins as a simple effort to move more can turn into something much deeper: a connection with yourself, a rhythm to your day, a feeling of lightness that goes beyond the physical.

In Summary

Walking is not just a way to move your body — it's a way to care for your entire self. It's accessible, adaptable, and incredibly effective. When you create a **walking habit for health and energy**, you begin to shift the way you feel in your body, your mind, and your life.

In the chapters ahead, we'll explore how to build a daily walking habit that works for you — with practical tools, mindset tips, and a 30-day challenge to get you moving. You don't need to be perfect. You don't need to be fast. You just need to be willing to take that first step.

So — shall we begin?

Chapter Two: Resetting Your Routine: How to Start and Keep Going

You don't need to wait for motivation to strike. You don't need a fancy plan or a perfect pair of shoes. To start a walking habit, all you need is the decision to begin — and the willingness to do it imperfectly.

In this chapter, we'll look at how to go from *thinking* about walking to actually doing it. You'll learn how to remove the most common barriers, set realistic goals, and make walking something you look forward to — rather than another thing on your to-do list.

This is about creating a **daily fitness routine for beginners** — something gentle, flexible, and effective enough to stick with.

Start Where You Are

There's no need to overhaul your life overnight. The best way to start walking regularly is to begin exactly where you are — with the time, energy and resources you currently have.

Ask yourself:

- When during the day do I feel most able to take a short break?

- Are there existing routines (school run, commute, errands) where I could walk instead of drive?

- Could I walk while listening to a podcast or making a phone call?

- Is there a safe, nearby route that feels accessible and pleasant?

This is about finding **simple walking habits for real life**, not ideal life. Even five minutes of walking is a great starting point. You can always add more later.

Set a Manageable Goal

One of the most effective ways to create any habit is to **set a clear, realistic goal**. For walking, that means choosing something that's:

- **Small** enough that you won't resist it
- **Specific** enough to track
- **Flexible** enough to fit around your lifestyle

Some great beginner goals might be:

- Walk for 10 minutes after lunch each weekday
- Walk 2,000 steps every day for a week
- Go for a short walk every morning before you check your phone
- Walk three times this week, even if it's just around the block

This isn't about proving anything. This is about **building consistency**, which matters more than intensity, duration, or step count in the early stages.

If you've searched for how to build a **daily walking habit for health and energy**, the answer begins with a goal you can meet — even on your tired or unmotivated days.

Make It Easy to Begin

The biggest challenge with any new habit isn't the doing — it's the *starting*. That moment when you decide to go for a walk or stay on the sofa. Here are a few simple ways to make starting easier:

- **Keep your walking shoes by the door** — a visual cue that reminds you to move

- **Lay out your clothes the night before** if you walk in the morning

- **Attach walking to an existing habit**, like having coffee or finishing a work call

- **Use a countdown**: "3-2-1, go" and stand up — you'll be surprised how often this works

The less effort it takes to begin, the more likely you are to follow through.

Track Progress — Without Obsession

One of the best ways to stay motivated is to see your own progress. But that doesn't mean you need a complicated app or a detailed spreadsheet. You can track your walking in whatever way feels good to you:

- A simple tick on a calendar

- A step count on your phone or smartwatch

- A notebook where you jot down the date and how the walk felt

- A habit tracker where you colour in boxes or fill out circles

If you're someone who enjoys numbers, feel free to use a pedometer or fitness app to track **steps for losing weight**, or distance. But if numbers make you feel pressured, focus instead on **how you feel after your walks**.

Remember: the real goal is building a habit that lasts — not hitting perfect numbers every day.

Make It Enjoyable

Let's be honest — you're far more likely to stick with something you enjoy. So don't treat walking like a punishment. Instead, make it something you look forward to.

Try these ideas:

- **Create a walking playlist** with upbeat or calming music

- **Listen to audiobooks or podcasts** while you walk

- **Explore different routes** — even short detours can make it feel fresh

- **Walk in nature** if possible — studies show it boosts mental health

- **Walk with a friend or dog** for companionship and accountability

- **Turn your walk into a mindfulness moment** — breathe deeply, notice your surroundings, let your thoughts settle

Walking doesn't need to be fast or fancy to be effective. The more positive emotion you associate with it, the more likely you are to repeat it.

Deal with Resistance Before It Wins

Everyone — *everyone* — hits a point where they just don't feel like walking. Maybe it's cold. Maybe you're tired. Maybe your day ran away from you.

The key isn't to avoid resistance. The key is to plan for it.

Ask yourself:

- What will I do when I don't feel like walking?

- Can I give myself permission to do just five minutes and then stop?

- Could I walk in place indoors, or up and down the hallway, just to stay consistent?

Building a strong **walking habit for mood and motivation** means being flexible and kind with yourself. The goal isn't perfection — it's showing up more often than not.

Create a Walking-Friendly Environment

Sometimes the best way to build a habit is to shape the world around you. Here's how to create a home and life that makes walking easier:

- Keep your walking shoes and coat visible and ready

- Have a designated walking route that's familiar and easy

- Let others in your household know your walking time is "you time"
- Use reminders or alarms to prompt you during the day
- Celebrate your wins — even small ones — with rewards or positive self-talk

Every small decision to support your habit adds up. Over time, it becomes part of your identity: "I'm someone who walks every day."

The Myth of Motivation

Let's clear something up: you do *not* need to feel motivated every day to walk.

Motivation is fleeting. Some days you'll have it, some days you won't. That's normal. The people who walk daily don't rely on motivation — they rely on routine.

They've built the habit into their day like brushing their teeth. Some days it feels magical. Other days it feels like a chore. But they do it anyway.

You can, too.

If you're building this as a **low impact exercise for busy adults**, your best strategy isn't waiting to feel inspired — it's designing a routine that carries you even when you're tired, distracted, or not in the mood.

Begin Today — However Small

If you've been waiting for the "right" time to start walking… this is it.

Not Monday. Not next month. Not when your schedule clears up or the weather improves. Start with the smallest possible action — a two-minute walk around your block, a stroll to the postbox, a few laps around the kitchen.

It doesn't have to be perfect to count.

Small steps become big change. One walk becomes a streak. A streak becomes a habit. A habit becomes a lifestyle.

In Summary

To build a daily walking routine:

- Start small and specific — focus on consistency, not intensity
- Make walking easy to begin — reduce friction and prepare cues
- Track your progress in a way that motivates you
- Choose routes and methods that feel enjoyable
- Expect resistance and have a plan for low-energy days
- Focus on building a habit, not chasing motivation

Every step you take reinforces a message: *I'm doing something good for myself.*

You don't need to become a different person. You just need to keep showing up — one step, one walk, one day at a time.

Chapter Three: The Mind-Body Reset: Calm, Clarity, and Confidence

When we think about exercise, we often picture physical results — weight loss, stronger muscles, improved heart health. But walking offers something deeper, something quieter, and in many ways, even more powerful: it supports your mind.

One of the most profound benefits of building a **daily walking habit for health and energy** is the effect it has on your mood, your mindset, and your mental clarity. Walking doesn't just move your body — it helps shift your perspective, quiet your stress, and reconnect you with yourself.

You may begin walking to feel better in your body, but what often surprises people is how much better it makes them feel in their mind.

The Science of Walking for Mental Health

Modern research has caught up with what many of us instinctively know: movement is medicine — not just for the body, but for the brain.

When you walk, your brain releases a cocktail of feel-good chemicals:

- **Endorphins**, which reduce pain and boost mood

- **Dopamine**, associated with motivation and pleasure

- **Serotonin**, which stabilises mood and supports emotional regulation

- **Brain-Derived Neurotrophic Factor (BDNF)**, which helps brain cells grow and repair

Even a short, gentle walk can reduce levels of **cortisol**, the body's main stress hormone. That's why many people who adopt a **walking exercise for mental wellness** report feeling less anxious, less irritable, and more emotionally resilient.

In fact, walking has been shown to be as effective as some forms of medication for mild to moderate depression, and it's often recommended by therapists and doctors as a first-line treatment for managing low mood, fatigue, and chronic stress.

The Power of Rhythm

Part of walking's magic lies in its rhythm. Step by step, breath by breath, it naturally helps regulate the nervous system.

Unlike high-intensity workouts that spike adrenaline, walking activates the **parasympathetic nervous system** — the body's "rest and digest" mode. It calms the heart rate, relaxes tense muscles, and signals safety to the brain.

This is especially important if you're often in **fight-or-flight** mode — rushing through life, juggling stress, or carrying emotional tension. A **daily fitness routine for beginners** like walking gives your nervous system a much-needed break.

Walking slows you down — not in a lazy way, but in a healing way. It invites you to breathe more deeply, notice your surroundings, and feel more present in your body.

Walking as Moving Meditation

You don't have to sit cross-legged or close your eyes to experience mindfulness. Walking, when done with intention, can be just as grounding.

Try this on your next walk:

- **Leave your phone behind**, or keep it in your pocket

- **Breathe in sync with your steps** — inhale for 4 steps, exhale for 4

- **Notice five things you can see**

- **Feel your feet connect with the ground**

- **Let your thoughts pass like clouds, without judgement**

This simple shift — from walking to *mindful* walking — helps reduce rumination and mental clutter. You don't need to *clear* your mind. You just need to give it space.

Many people describe walking as a form of "moving meditation," and for good reason. It's one of the easiest ways to feel both grounded and free at the same time.

Clear Thinking, Better Decisions

Have you ever noticed how ideas seem to come more easily when you're walking? That's not a coincidence.

Walking increases blood flow to the brain, which supports creativity, memory, and problem-solving. In fact, a well-known study at Stanford University found that walking boosted creative thinking by up to 60% compared to sitting.

That's why many writers, inventors, and entrepreneurs swear by their daily walks. Steve Jobs was famous for holding "walking meetings." Charles Dickens reportedly walked miles every day to clear his mind and dream up new characters.

You don't have to be a genius to benefit. If you're feeling stuck, scattered or foggy, a brisk 10-minute walk can be more effective than staring at your screen or pouring another coffee.

Emotional Healing, Step by Step

There's something profoundly healing about moving forward — physically and emotionally.

Walking helps you process thoughts and emotions without needing to analyse or explain them. It gives you a safe, neutral space to reflect — or simply *be*. For many people, walking becomes a daily mental reset, a chance to release tension, replay conversations, or let go of whatever the day has brought.

If you've experienced burnout, grief, or a difficult life season, walking can be part of your recovery. There's no pressure to perform, no scoreboard to beat — just your feet, your breath, and the simple act of carrying yourself forward.

It's why many people use walking as a cornerstone in their emotional self-care routines. It's not just movement — it's a message: *I'm showing up for myself today.*

Walking to Reduce Stress and Anxiety

Stress and anxiety often live in the body: tight shoulders, shallow breathing, a racing mind. And because walking is a full-body movement, it helps *release* that tension physically as well as mentally.

Even a short walk can:

- Help regulate breathing and reduce the physical symptoms of anxiety
- Provide a change of environment, which breaks negative thought loops
- Lower muscle tension and increase oxygen flow
- Create a feeling of movement and progress, even if the problem isn't solved

If you're someone who tends to overthink, worry or spiral into "what ifs," walking offers a way out — not necessarily with answers, but with space and perspective.

It's one of the most accessible ways to **reduce stress and anxiety naturally**, and it costs nothing but your time.

Walking and Confidence

Here's something you might not expect: walking can boost your confidence — not just because of weight loss or fitness, but because of the habit itself.

Each time you follow through on your walk, you send a subtle but powerful message to yourself: *I keep my promises. I take care of myself. I can do hard things.*

That builds **self-trust**, which is the foundation of confidence. And as you walk more, you start to feel stronger, more capable, and more in control of your day.

You may find yourself walking taller — literally and figuratively. You'll start noticing how good it feels to move with purpose. You may begin dressing with more ease, speaking with more clarity, or showing up more fully in other areas of your life.

It doesn't happen overnight. But it *does* happen — one walk, one step, one choice at a time.

How to Maximise the Mental Benefits

To get the most from walking for your mind and mood:

- **Walk outdoors whenever possible** — natural light and greenery enhance the effects
- **Ditch multitasking sometimes** — allow your brain to slow down
- **Use your walk as a "transition zone"** between work and home
- **Reflect on how you feel afterwards** — mentally and emotionally
- **Be consistent** — even short walks done daily have long-lasting effects

Your walk doesn't have to be perfect. It just has to happen.

In Summary

Walking is one of the simplest ways to care for your mental health. It helps reduce stress, ease anxiety, improve focus, and boost your mood — all while supporting your physical wellbeing. It reconnects you to yourself, clears your head, and creates a sense of calm confidence that lasts far beyond the walk itself.

You don't need to meditate, journal, or "fix" anything to benefit. Just step outside, breathe deeply, and let your body and mind move in harmony.

Chapter Four: Making Your Walk a Daily Joy

One of the most important — and most overlooked — parts of building a sustainable walking habit is **enjoyment**. If your walk feels like a chore, something you have to *force* yourself to do every day, chances are you won't stick with it for long.

The people who walk every day aren't necessarily more disciplined — they're just more attached to the **pleasure** they get from it. And you can be, too.

This chapter is all about helping you fall in love with walking — or at the very least, like it enough to keep showing up.

Don't Just Walk — Make It Yours

Walking is highly customisable. You can walk fast or slow, long or short. You can walk with music, in silence, or with a friend. You can walk in nature or around your block. You can even **turn a simple walk into a moment of calm, clarity or creativity**.

This flexibility is what makes walking such a perfect **low impact exercise for busy adults** — and it's also what gives you the chance to shape it into something that fits your lifestyle and personality.

Ask yourself:

- What would make walking feel more like a treat than a task?

- What can I add (or subtract) to make it more enjoyable?

- Where do I feel most peaceful or refreshed when I walk?

Now, let's explore some simple ways to make walking something you genuinely look forward to.

Add Sound: Music, Podcasts and Audiobooks

Many people find walking far more enjoyable with something to listen to — and thankfully, there's no shortage of options.

- **Upbeat music** can energise your pace and mood

- **Calm music** can help you unwind

- **Podcasts** can make your walk feel like a productive use of time

- **Audiobooks** turn your daily walk into Storytime

You can even build your own **"walking playlist"** — music that gets you out the door and keeps you moving. Spotify, Apple Music and YouTube are full of curated walking playlists to explore.

If you're building a **daily fitness routine for beginners**, pairing your walk with something enjoyable helps build a positive emotional association — which is key for long-term success.

Tip: If you tend to overthink or feel mentally cluttered, music or spoken audio can give your mind something to focus on, creating a light, meditative state.

Add Nature: The Green Effect

Walking outdoors, especially in green spaces, brings **extra mental and physical benefits**. Research shows that walking in nature:

- Lowers stress levels more effectively than urban walking

- Reduces symptoms of anxiety and depression

- Improves focus and memory

- Boosts immune function

- Elevates mood

Even a **short walk in a park, near trees, or by water** can help reset your nervous system and give you a greater sense of calm. It's no wonder many people describe walking in nature as therapeutic.

You don't need access to a forest. Even a leafy neighbourhood, a garden path, or a riverbank can create the **nature connection** your mind and body crave.

Add Variety: Shake Up Your Routine

Doing the exact same walk every day can get boring — and boredom is one of the top reasons people abandon otherwise healthy habits. The good news? Walking is endlessly adaptable.

Try mixing it up with:

- **Different routes**: Explore new paths, parks, streets or trails

- **Different times of day**: A morning walk feels different to an evening one

- **Different purposes**: Some days walk to reflect, other days to energise
- **Different companions**: Walk alone, with a friend, or even with your dog

Creating a walking routine doesn't mean walking the same route at the same speed every single day. The **habit is in the doing**, not in the details.

When you give yourself permission to experiment, you keep the habit fresh — and your brain engaged.

Add Companionship: People and Pets

Walking can be a wonderful solo ritual — but it can also be a deeply social one.

Invite a friend or neighbour to walk with you once a week. It doesn't have to be a long or intense catch-up. Even a gentle walk-and-talk can boost connection and make the time fly by.

If you have a dog, you already have the perfect accountability partner. Dogs love routine, and many walkers say their dog actually *gets them out the door* on days they otherwise wouldn't have moved.

Bonus: When you walk with someone else, you're far more likely to stay consistent — even when motivation dips.

Add Purpose: Walking as "You Time"

In busy adult life, it's easy to feel like you're constantly doing things *for* other people — work, kids, partners, responsibilities. Walking gives you a chance to take a **small slice of the day back for yourself**.

Treat your walk as:

- A mental reset
- A boundary between work and home
- A transition between two parts of your day
- A reward for completing a task
- A time to clear your head or let ideas flow

You don't need to walk to burn calories or "earn" your lunch. You can walk simply because it helps you feel like yourself again.

Creating **simple walking habits for real life** means building the walk *into* your lifestyle — not trying to squeeze your lifestyle around a rigid fitness plan.

Add Repetition: Building Positive Association

There's a reason people talk about the "habit loop": the more often you do something that feels good, the more your brain wants to do it again.

The trick? **Repeat the conditions that make the walk enjoyable**.

That could mean:

- Walking at the same time every day
- Starting with your favourite song
- Walking the same loop until it becomes second nature
- Ending your walk with a cup of tea or a short rest

30

The more positive emotion you link to walking, the easier it becomes to return to the habit. You're creating not just a routine, but a **ritual** — a moment that belongs to you.

What About Bad Weather?

The weather can be a challenge. But walking doesn't have to stop just because it's raining or cold.

Here's how to walk more comfortably year-round:

- **Invest in a decent waterproof jacket and walking shoes**
- **Keep a towel or spare shoes near the door**
- **Try short indoor walks**: around the house, at the supermarket, or on the spot
- **Remind yourself how good you'll feel afterwards**

Some people even grow to love walking in light rain or cool weather — it can feel refreshing, invigorating, and oddly peaceful.

The key is preparation. A little discomfort is worth the long-term gain.

In Summary

Making your walking habit enjoyable is one of the **most powerful ways to make it last**. When your walk becomes something you *look forward to*, the need for motivation fades — and it becomes something you naturally protect and prioritise.

Here's how to keep it enjoyable:

- Add music, podcasts or audiobooks

- Walk in nature whenever possible

- Mix up your routes, times or goals

- Walk with a friend or your dog

- Treat it as your personal time — not another obligation

- Repeat what feels good, and ditch what doesn't

- Be kind to yourself on days that don't go perfectly

There is no "right" way to walk — only the way that keeps you coming back. The more you enjoy the process, the more it becomes part of your life.

Chapter Five: Tracking Your Reset — Without Pressure or Perfection

Most people set goals and never follow through. Not because they don't care — but because they lose track. They forget to celebrate small wins, can't see how far they've come, and give up long before results appear.

This is where tracking comes in — not as a rigid numbers game, but as a gentle tool to help you **stay connected to your habit**. When it comes to building a daily walking routine, tracking your progress helps keep the momentum alive.

The key is to do it in a way that works for *you* — encouraging, not punishing. Flexible, not obsessive.

In this chapter, we'll explore:

- The psychology of why tracking works

- What to track and how to do it

- How to stay consistent without becoming perfectionist

- What to do when you fall off track

- And how to use tracking to deepen your self-awareness and motivation

Let's begin.

Why Track At All?

There's an old saying in productivity circles: *what gets measured gets managed*. But when it comes to wellness habits like walking, we're not just measuring numbers — we're reinforcing identity.

Tracking:

- Builds self-awareness: "How often am I actually walking?"

- Reinforces consistency: "I've walked four days this week — I'm on a roll."

- Creates motivation: "Look how far I've come since I started."

- Gives you a visual reward loop: seeing progress *feels* good

- Keeps your habit present in your mind

Most of all, it helps turn walking from a vague intention into a grounded, repeatable behaviour.

You're not just *trying* to walk regularly — you *are* walking regularly. You have the evidence to prove it.

What Should You Track?

You don't need to track everything. In fact, the simpler your system, the more likely you are to use it consistently.

Here are the most useful things you might want to track in your walking habit:

Days Walked

This is the simplest metric. Did you walk today — yes or no? Tick the day off. Easy.

Duration

How long did you walk? This can be tracked in minutes, which is more relatable than miles.

Steps Taken

If you have a smartwatch or phone, track your steps. 5,000–10,000 is a popular goal, but even 2,000 steps can be a great start. This suits those focused on a **walking plan for weight loss or overall energy**.

Time of Day

Morning, lunch break, after dinner — noting when you walk helps you find patterns that work.

Mood Before and After

This is incredibly powerful. Tracking how you feel before and after helps your brain associate walking with emotional rewards.

Notes or Reflections

Some people like to jot a few words: "Felt good," "Tired today," "Walked in the rain," "Listened to a brilliant podcast." These details make your journey more personal and engaging.

You don't need to track all of these. Pick one to start with — maybe just ticking off the days — and build from there.

How to Track Without Overthinking

There are many ways to track your walking habit. Choose the one that fits your personality and lifestyle best.

Paper Tracker

The classic method. Use a calendar, planner, or printable habit tracker. Colour in boxes. Cross off days. Seeing your streak grow is a powerful motivator.

Habit Tracking Apps

Apps like Streaks, Done, Habitica or HabitBull are great for tracking yes/no habits. Most are customisable, visual and give reminders.

Step Counter Apps

Your phone likely has a built-in pedometer. Apple Health, Google Fit, and Fitbit apps track daily step count and walking distance. This works well for those motivated by metrics.

Walking Journal

Keep a small notebook or digital journal. Write down your mood, route, weather, and a short reflection. This is ideal if you enjoy mindfulness or want to notice subtle changes.

The "Sticky Note" Method

Low-tech but effective. Stick a note on your fridge or desk with 30 blank boxes. Each walk, tick one off.

It's not about finding the best system. It's about finding one that feels natural — one you'll actually use.

What Counts as a "Walk"?

Let's clear something up: **every walk counts**.

Don't fall into the trap of thinking your walk "didn't count" because it was short, slow or casual. That thinking leads to guilt and discouragement — the two things that kill habits.

Whether you walked five minutes around the block, 20 minutes with your dog, or did laps around the kitchen while on the phone — it all counts. You moved. You kept the habit alive.

The most powerful walking habits are built on **flexibility**, not perfectionism.

How to Stay Consistent

Consistency doesn't mean walking every day without fail. It means returning to your habit again and again, even after busy days, tired weeks, or disrupted routines.

Here's how to build that kind of resilience:

Link Walking to an Identity

Instead of saying, "I need to walk," say: "I'm someone who walks every day." Your actions begin to align with your identity.

Use Triggers and Cues

Attach your walk to something else you already do:

- After breakfast = walk
- Before work = walk
- End of lunch = walk
- After dinner = walk

Habits stick best when they're anchored to routines that already exist.

Build the Chain

Tracking creates visual momentum — and momentum drives motivation. The more days in a row you walk, the more you *want* to keep going.

Even a 5-minute walk "keeps the chain alive."

What If You Miss a Day?

You will miss days. It's not failure — it's reality.

When that happens:

- Don't make it mean anything. It's just a blip.
- Avoid the "all or nothing" trap: missing one day doesn't cancel your habit
- Walk the next day — even just a few minutes — and move on
- Reflect gently: "What got in the way?" "How can I adjust tomorrow?"

If tracking ever feels like guilt or pressure, scale it back. The goal is progress, not punishment.

When Tracking Doesn't Work

Some people find that tracking becomes obsessive. They feel anxious if they don't hit a certain number of steps or miss a day on their tracker.

If that's you, **simplify**. Focus on:

- Mood-based tracking: "Did I feel better after?"
- Frequency over streaks: "I walked four times this week. That's a win."
- Gentle journaling: "What worked today? What didn't?"

Always remember: walking is here to support you — not control you. If tracking gets in the way of that, change your system.

Celebrate Your Wins

You might not get a certificate for walking three times a week for a month — but you *should*. That's progress. That's commitment. That's health being built one step at a time.

Try:

- Acknowledge your consistency: "Look at me showing up."

- Share your wins with a friend or group

- Treat yourself with something joyful: a new audiobook, a fresh pair of socks, a walk in a new place

Walking is an act of self-respect. Honour it.

Journaling Prompt (Optional)

"What has tracking my walking habit taught me about myself?"

Use this to reflect on patterns, mindset, and shifts in mood or energy. Sometimes the walk is just the beginning — the insight comes afterwards.

In Summary

Tracking is not about pressure — it's about awareness. It helps you stay connected to your walking habit, celebrate your progress, and recover more easily when life gets in the way.

Start simple. Be flexible. Focus on what feels good.

And remember: the most powerful habits are the ones you enjoy enough to come back to — again and again.

Chapter Six: Walking Through Real Life: Resetting in Hard Moments

It's easy to start a walking habit when life is calm, the weather is mild, and your motivation is high. But let's be honest — life isn't always calm, the weather isn't always kind, and motivation doesn't always show up.

That's where many people get stuck.

But here's the good news: **you don't need perfect conditions to be consistent**. You just need to anticipate the common challenges and know how to move through them. Consistency isn't about never missing a day. It's about coming back — again and again — even when it's messy, inconvenient or hard.

This chapter is your practical toolkit for staying on track, even in real life — with its interruptions, tired days, and unpredictable demands.

Let's break it down.

Challenge #1: "I Don't Have Time"

This is the number one excuse — and a very real feeling for many people. Between work, family, chores, and all the invisible tasks of modern life, it can feel like there's simply *no space* for a walk.

But here's the thing: walking doesn't require a massive time block. You don't need an hour. You don't even need 30 minutes. Most of the time, what you need is a mindset shift.

Try This:

- **Break it into bits**: 5 minutes before breakfast, 5 at lunch, 5 after dinner = 15 minutes total.

- **Replace time-wasters**: Could you swap 10 minutes of scrolling or TV for a short walk?

- **Walk with purpose**: Combine your walk with errands, phone calls, or school runs.

- **Schedule it**: Put it in your calendar like a meeting — even if it's just 10 minutes.

Short walks *count*. A few minutes is better than nothing. A quick pace around your home is better than skipping altogether. This is a habit for real life — and real life is busy. So be flexible. You don't need a chunk of time; you need the choice to use small pockets well.

Challenge #2: "I'm Too Tired"

Sometimes the last thing you want to do is go for a walk. You're exhausted — physically, mentally, emotionally. And the idea of adding one more thing to your plate feels impossible.

But here's the paradox: **walking gives energy**. It gently boosts circulation, oxygenates your brain, and helps clear mental fatigue. It's one of the most accessible ways to re-energise — without caffeine or sugar.

Try This:

- **Lower the bar**: Tell yourself, "Just five minutes." Most of the time, once you're up and moving, you'll feel more awake.

- **Walk slowly**: Not every walk has to be brisk or intense. A slow, mindful walk is still movement.

- **Track how you feel afterwards**: Often you'll notice you're *less* tired post-walk than before.

Energy isn't always a prerequisite for walking. Sometimes, it's the result.

Challenge #3: "The Weather's Terrible"

Ah, the British classic. Rain. Wind. Cold. Grey skies. It's no surprise that weather is one of the most common reasons people skip their walks. But with the right mindset — and a few practical tweaks — you can walk in most conditions.

Tips for Wet or Cold Days:

- **Invest in a good waterproof coat and sturdy shoes**

- **Carry a compact umbrella or wear a hood**

- **Layer up — warmth = comfort**

- **Walk shorter but still walk — five minutes counts**

- **Try mall walking, museum walking or stair walking**

- **Walk indoors — around the house, in place, or up and down the stairs**

Remember: You don't need ideal weather. You need a habit that's stronger than your excuse.

Some walkers actually *grow to love* walking in light rain or cool air. It's quiet. Calming. A chance to feel refreshed.

You might not enjoy every minute — but you'll always be glad you did it.

Challenge #4: "I'm Not Seeing Results"

We live in a world of instant feedback — likes, stats, step counts, and progress pictures. So when we don't see big changes fast, it's easy to get discouraged.

But the truth is, **the most powerful results from walking are often invisible at first**:

- Improved mood
- Better sleep
- Reduced stress
- Clearer thinking
- More energy during the day
- A subtle shift in how you feel in your body

These are *quiet wins* — but they matter deeply. They're the foundation for everything else.

If weight loss or physical change is your focus, remind yourself: **walking is a long game**. And the changes are happening, even if they're not visible yet.

Try This:

- Keep a "feelings log" for two weeks — note your mood, energy, and sleep
- Celebrate non-scale victories: looser clothes, more confidence, better focus
- Avoid comparison: walking is *your* journey, at *your* pace

The results are happening. Keep going.

Challenge #5: "I Get Bored"

Boredom is a habit-killer. If your walk always looks and feels the same, your mind will start to rebel. But the great thing about walking is that it's infinitely adaptable.

Add Variety:

- Change your route or direction
- Walk at a different time of day
- Listen to a new podcast or audiobook
- Walk with a friend or dog
- Add a purpose (errand, call, thinking time)
- Set a challenge: "How many trees can I spot?" "How many steps in 10 mins?"

Remember: **novelty fuels motivation**. When you mix it up, you stay engaged — and your brain stays interested.

Challenge #6: "I Lost My Streak"

You were doing so well. Walking every day. Tracking it. Feeling good. And then... life happened. You got sick. Work got stressful. The weather was awful. One missed walk turned into two... then three.

Now you feel like you've blown it. Like the habit's broken. Like you'll have to start all over again.

Sound familiar?

This is the perfection trap. And it's one of the biggest threats to long-term consistency.

But here's the truth: **missing a few days doesn't ruin your habit — giving up does**.

Reframe It:

- You didn't "fail." You paused.

- You're not "starting over." You're *continuing* — this is part of the journey.

- Every comeback walk makes your habit stronger, not weaker.

The best walkers aren't perfect — they're persistent.

Challenge #7: "I Feel Self-Conscious"

Some people worry about how they look when they walk. Maybe you feel uncomfortable in workout clothes. Or embarrassed to walk alone. Or judged by others in public spaces.

First: you are not alone in this. Many people — especially beginners — feel some form of walking anxiety.

But here's what matters: **your walk is not for them. It's for you.**

Mindset Shifts:

- Most people are too busy with their own lives to notice you

- You're doing something good for your health and happiness — that's worth celebrating

- You don't need the "right" clothes — just comfortable shoes and weather-appropriate layers

- If it helps, wear sunglasses, headphones, or walk in quieter areas

Your courage to show up — even while feeling awkward — is what builds confidence.

Challenge #8: "I Just Don't Feel Like It"

Ah, motivation. The unreliable friend. Sometimes you have it, sometimes you don't. And if you only walk when you *feel* like it... well, you'll walk occasionally.

But here's the thing: **consistency is built on commitment, not emotion**.

You don't need to *want* to walk. You just need to *decide* to.

Strategies for Low-Motivation Days:

- Shrink the task: "Just two minutes"

- Use habit stacking: "After tea, I walk"

- Remind yourself: "I never regret a walk"

- Say: "I'll just put on my shoes" — and see what happens

- Repeat your WHY: energy, calm, confidence, health

Action leads to motivation — not the other way around.

The Real Secret: Make the Habit Forgiving

The most successful walking habits aren't the most intense — they're the most **forgiving**.

They bend when life gets chaotic. They flex around your mood. They pause for a sick day and restart without drama.

They survive because you've removed the guilt, shame and unrealistic expectations. You've allowed yourself to be human — and to keep walking anyway.

That's the habit that lasts.

Quick Recap: Your Walking Toolkit for Real Life

Challenge	Solution
No time	Break it into small bursts, multitask, walk with purpose
Too tired	Walk slowly, use it to boost energy, try 5 mins only
Bad weather	Prepare well, walk indoors, walk short but still walk
No visible results	Focus on mood/energy/sleep — the hidden wins
Boredom	Mix it up: route, time, audio, purpose
Lost momentum	Reframe: restart, don't punish, keep going
Feel self-conscious	Own your walk, dress for you, find quiet spaces
Low motivation	Act first — motivation will catch up

Final Thought

Walking doesn't need perfection. It needs patience.

There will be off days. Busy weeks. Setbacks. Skipped walks. All of that is part of the process — not a failure of it.

The question is not "How do I walk every single day without missing a beat?"
It's "How do I build a habit I return to, again and again, no matter what?"

Now you have your answer.

Chapter Seven: Real Resets: Walking Stories from
Everyday Lives

It's one thing to read about the benefits of walking in
theory. It's another thing entirely to hear how real people
— with real jobs, families, challenges and busy lives —
have built walking into their routines and changed their
wellbeing in meaningful ways.

These aren't elite athletes or influencers. They're ordinary
people who decided to take one small step, and then
another, until walking became part of who they are.

In this chapter, you'll meet a handful of individuals who
started where you are. Each of their stories shows a
different angle of the walking journey: health, energy,
emotional healing, confidence, connection, and more.

You might see yourself in one of them. Or a bit of all of
them.

Clare, 52 — From Overwhelmed to Empowered

"I used to wake up and immediately feel behind. I'd reach
for my phone, check emails, scroll the news — and I'd
already be stressed before I even got out of bed.

One day I thought, 'What if I started my mornings
differently?' I decided to take a short walk before
touching any screens. Just ten minutes. No phone. No
agenda.

At first it felt strange. But after a few days, I noticed I was
less reactive and more focused. I started looking forward
to that quiet space.

Now, I walk for about 25 minutes each morning — rain or shine. It sets the tone for my whole day. I feel like I'm leading my morning, not chasing it."

What worked for Clare: Linking walking to an existing routine, prioritising mindset, keeping it screen-free.

Simon, 45 — Weight Loss Without the Gym

"I'd gained a lot of weight over the years — mostly from working long hours, eating on the go, and never really exercising. I always thought I needed to join a gym to fix it, but I hated the idea.

Then I read somewhere that walking every day could help. It sounded too simple, but I figured I had nothing to lose.

I started walking in the evenings after work — just 15 minutes to begin with. Then I added music. Then I started noticing how much better I felt — lighter, calmer.

Six months later, I'd lost over a stone and was walking 45 minutes most days. But more importantly, I felt like myself again. I didn't dread movement anymore. I craved it."

What worked for Simon: Starting small, attaching walks to the end of his workday, tracking progress without pressure.

Priya, 38 — Walking for Mental Clarity

"My anxiety had been building for years. Work stress, family demands, always being 'on'. I struggled to sleep, overthought everything, and constantly felt on edge.

My therapist suggested daily walking — not for fitness, but as a kind of moving meditation. I was sceptical, but desperate.

I started walking after dinner each evening. No phone. Just me, my breath, and the sound of my steps.

It was weirdly powerful. Like the rhythm soothed something in me. Over time, I noticed I wasn't snapping at people as much. I slept more deeply. I felt more grounded.

Walking hasn't 'cured' my anxiety — but it's one of my strongest tools now."

What worked for Priya: Creating a peaceful, consistent walking ritual, walking without tech, using breath and rhythm to self-regulate.

Megan and James, 60s — Connection Through Walking

"We retired within six months of each other, and suddenly found ourselves under the same roof, all day, every day. It was... an adjustment.

One evening, after a tense afternoon over something ridiculous, James said, 'Let's go for a walk.'

We walked in silence for ten minutes. Then we started talking — properly. Without phones. Without distraction. Just walking and talking.

It became a habit — our post-dinner walk. Some nights we chat about the day. Others we just walk in comfortable silence.

It's helped our health, yes. But even more than that, it's helped our marriage."

What worked for Megan and James: Using walking as a space to reconnect, a gentle ritual for communication and togetherness.

Yusuf, 29 — Breaking Out of Burnout

"I work in finance, and like a lot of people in my industry, I was hitting burnout hard. Long hours. Sitting all day. Living on energy drinks. I felt awful — mentally foggy, physically tense, emotionally drained.

A colleague told me he started walking during his lunch breaks, and it helped reset his mind. I tried it.

I walked for 20 minutes at noon every day. At first it felt like a waste of time — I thought I should be working. But then I realised I came back to my desk clearer, calmer, and actually *more* productive.

Now I protect that time fiercely. It's non-negotiable. No meetings. No multitasking. Just me, fresh air, and my sanity."

What worked for Yusuf: Scheduling walks during the workday, noticing improved focus and productivity, treating walking as a boundary.

Lara, 35 — From Sedentary to Steady

"I hated exercise. I always felt awkward, slow, and out of place. But after two pregnancies and years of desk work, my back ached constantly and I had no stamina.

I didn't want to join a gym, so I started walking while pushing the pram. I made a rule: walk every day, even if it was just to the end of the road and back.

Some days I only managed five minutes. Other days I got to the park and back. Slowly, it added up. My back stopped hurting. I felt steadier, stronger. And for once, I wasn't exercising to punish my body — I was walking to *support* it."

What worked for Lara: Releasing perfectionism, embracing gentle movement, staying consistent with a flexible standard.

What These Stories Have in Common

Despite their different backgrounds, goals, and situations, these walkers all did a few key things:

1. Started Small and Stayed Flexible

No one began with a perfect plan or long walk. They started where they were — often with just five or ten minutes — and built up slowly.

2. Connected Walking to a Personal "Why"

They weren't walking just because they "should." They were walking to feel better. To calm down. To clear their head. To reconnect. To heal. That kind of motivation runs deep.

3. Turned Walking into a Ritual

Whether it was a morning reset, a lunchtime boundary, or an evening wind-down, they walked at roughly the same time each day — creating rhythm, reliability, and emotional reward.

4. Made It Theirs

Some walked in silence. Others listened to music or walked with partners. Some tracked steps, others focused on feeling. They all found a way to make walking *fit them*, not the other way around.

Your Turn

You don't need a dramatic story or perfect plan to get started. All you need is a willingness to take the first few steps.

The power of walking lies in its accessibility — and its ability to meet you exactly where you are.

You might be like Clare, needing calm in the chaos.
Or like Darren, looking to improve your physical health.
Maybe you're like Priya, ready to manage stress with more care.
Or Yusuf, who uses walking to protect his energy.

Whatever your reason, it's valid. And your journey will be your own.

But one thing is certain: the benefits of walking multiply with each day you return to it.

Journaling Prompt (Optional)

"Whose story resonated most with me — and why?
What can I borrow from their approach to help shape my own walking routine?"

Write freely. No right answers — just reflection.

Final Thought

We often think transformation has to be big, bold, or Instagram-worthy. But more often than not, real change looks like a pair of trainers by the door. A walk after breakfast. A quiet decision to move forward — even on a grey day.

Walking isn't just about fitness. It's about feeling. Identity. Ownership. Empowerment.

And every time you choose to walk — especially when it would've been easier not to — you're writing your own story.

One step at a time.

Chapter Eight: The 30-Day Walking Reset Challenge

By now, you've read the science. You've explored the mindset. You've learned how to build consistency, overcome resistance, and make walking enjoyable.

But knowledge alone doesn't change your life — **action does**. That's where this challenge comes in.

The **30-Day Walking Habit Challenge** is designed to help you put everything you've learned into practice. One walk at a time. One day at a time.

It's not about pushing yourself to the limit. It's not about streaks or speed or step goals. It's about **building a realistic, repeatable walking habit** — something sustainable, enjoyable and deeply rooted in your real life.

Let's begin.

Why 30 Days?

Research into habit formation shows that while the average time to build a habit is 66 days, **the first 30 days are the most critical**. This is when you're laying the psychological groundwork:

- Creating triggers and routines
- Building emotional rewards
- Developing resilience against excuses
- Establishing identity — "I'm someone who walks"

Thirty days is long enough to experience real change, but short enough to feel doable.

It's not about walking perfectly for 30 days. It's about walking **often enough** for it to begin to feel natural — something you do because it *feels right*, not because you're forcing it.

How the Challenge Works

- **You will walk every day for the next 30 days**
- You choose the time, the pace, the route
- Start with small, easy wins
- Focus on consistency, not intensity
- Track your walks (using any method you like)
- Reflect once a week on how you're feeling
- Adjust the challenge to suit *your* life

You can use the printable tracker in the back of this book, your own calendar, or a habit tracking app.

If you miss a day — don't quit. Just start again the next day. This is a *forgiving* challenge, not a perfect one.

What Counts as a Walk?

Anything where you're on your feet, moving with intention.

- 5-minute stroll?
- Power walk around the park?
- Walking laps in your kitchen during a phone call?
- Dog walk, school run on foot, walk to the shop?

It all counts.

Suggested Structure: Week by Week

These are optional — feel free to follow or modify them.

Week 1: Getting Started (Days 1–7)

Goal: Show up daily, build the rhythm.

Focus on short, achievable walks. 5–15 minutes is perfect. Don't aim to impress. Aim to *start*.

- Choose a regular walking time
- Put your walking shoes by the door
- Pick a route or two that feels safe and simple
- Celebrate each day with a tick, smile or journal note

Mindset: You're not trying to do it all — you're trying to do *something* each day.

Week 2: Finding Flow (Days 8–14)

Goal: Build consistency, explore enjoyment.

Now that your habit has some traction, explore ways to make it more enjoyable.

- Try music, podcasts, or walking in nature
- Walk slightly longer if energy allows
- Reflect on how you feel after each walk
- Begin linking walking to emotional rewards (calm, focus, reset)

Mindset: It's not about willpower. It's about *positive association*.

Week 3: Building Resilience (Days 15–21)

Goal: Stick with it through the messy middle.

This is when motivation often dips. Life may get in the way. That's okay. This is your chance to practise *gentle persistence*.

- Walk shorter if needed, but still walk

- Mix up your routes or time of day

- Notice if resistance shows up — and walk through it anyway

- Reflect weekly: "What's working?" "What needs adjusting?"

Mindset: Keep it light. Keep it real. Just keep going.

Week 4: Owning the Habit (Days 22–30)

Goal: Feel the shift — from action to identity.

By now, walking may feel more automatic. Less effortful. More like part of who you are.

- Walk at your preferred time, with your preferred style

- Track mood, energy and confidence — what's changed?

- Celebrate your wins, no matter how small

- Think about how you want to continue beyond 30 days

Mindset: You're not building a challenge. You're building a way of life.

Daily Tracker Example

Here's a simple format to track each day:

Day	Duration	Mood Before	Mood After	Notes
1	10 mins	Tired	Clearer	Walked around the block, listened to birds
2	15 mins	Flat	Lighter	Tried a new route, felt proud
3	5 mins	Rushed	Still rushed, but glad I walked	Quick one before work

You can use a notebook, journal, spreadsheet, or phone app. Just pick one format and stick with it for 30 days.

Journal Prompts (Optional)

Use these once a week or whenever you feel stuck:

1. **What's changed since I began walking daily?**

2. **When do I enjoy walking the most? Why?**

3. **What has surprised me about myself during this challenge?**

4. **How has walking affected my energy, sleep, mood or mindset?**

5. **What do I want to take forward after Day 30?**

Frequently Asked Questions

What if I miss a day?

No guilt. No punishment. Pick up the next day and keep going. The habit survives because you *return*, not because you never miss.

Can I walk indoors?

Absolutely. Walk around your home, on the spot, or use a walking video online. Movement is what matters.

Can I walk more than once a day?

Yes! Bonus walks are great. But focus on consistency over quantity. One solid walk is better than an occasional long one.

Is it okay to walk slowly?

Yes. The pace is not important. What matters is that you walk with intention and attention.

How do I keep it up after 30 days?

Reflect, adjust, and recommit. Consider a new 30-day cycle with slightly longer walks or new routes. Or simply continue with what's working.

What to Expect by Day 30

If you stay consistent — even imperfectly — here's what you may notice by the end of this challenge:

- Greater energy during the day

- Less stress or mental clutter

- Better sleep

- A clearer mind and calmer emotions

- Improved confidence and self-trust

- A sense of rhythm and purpose

- More time spent outdoors and less on screens

- The beginning of a long-term walking habit

And perhaps most importantly: you'll feel proud. Not for walking perfectly, but for showing up consistently. For choosing something that supports your body and mind.

Celebrate!

When you finish the 30-Day Walking Habit Challenge:

- Acknowledge your effort

- Reflect on what you've learned

- Share your story if you feel comfortable (socially or privately)

- Reward yourself with something that supports your journey — new socks, a book, a quiet walk somewhere special

The reward doesn't have to be big — but it should feel meaningful.

You've earned it.

In Summary

The 30-Day Walking Habit Challenge is a starting point — not a finish line. It's here to help you:

- Build consistency
- Find enjoyment
- Navigate challenges
- Create emotional rewards
- Lay the foundation for a lifelong habit

No matter how small your steps, they matter. Because each one is a declaration: *I care about myself enough to move.*

You don't need perfection. You don't need to hit 10,000 steps. You don't need to feel motivated every day.

You just need to walk — one day at a time. One step at a time. One choice at a time.

Final Reflections: Walking as a Lifelong Reset

When you began reading this book, you may have simply wanted to move more, feel better, or create a healthier routine. Maybe you were feeling low on energy, high on stress, or just disconnected from your body.

And now, here you are.

Perhaps you've already started walking regularly. Perhaps you've completed the 30-day challenge. Or maybe you're still gently building your rhythm, one step at a time.

Wherever you are in your journey, I want to say this: **you're doing something important**. Far more important than most people realise.

Because walking — while simple — holds the power to shift everything.

It's Not Just a Habit — It's a Homecoming

We often think that getting healthy requires huge effort. Expensive gym memberships. Strict diets. High-tech trackers. Complex plans.

But walking reminds us of something essential: we don't always need to *add more*. Sometimes we need to return to what we already have.

Our legs.
Our breath.
Our ability to take one step — and then another.

Walking brings us back to ourselves. It slows us down in a world that rushes. It grounds us when our minds are scattered. It offers movement without pressure, progress without comparison, and strength without strain.

It's a habit. But it's also a kind of homecoming.

You've Built More Than a Routine

If you've walked regularly — even imperfectly — over the past few weeks or months, you've done more than get some steps in. You've built a foundation.

Here's what you've really done:

- Created time for yourself in a busy world
- Strengthened your mind-body connection
- Built resilience by walking even on low-energy days
- Shifted your identity from "someone who tries" to "someone who does"
- Created a healthy habit based on kindness, not punishment
- Discovered your own rhythm, preferences, and pace

These are wins worth celebrating. Quiet wins, perhaps — but the kind that transform lives over time.

Walking Changes More Than Just Your Health

Yes, walking can improve your heart, lungs, joints, digestion, and energy. But its reach goes further.

Walking also:

- Boosts confidence and self-trust

- Increases creative thinking and clarity

- Regulates emotions and reduces anxiety

- Encourages daily reflection and awareness

- Reconnects you with the outdoors and the present moment

- Restores a sense of rhythm to days that feel chaotic

In a very real way, walking helps you **feel more like yourself** again.

The Next Step: Make It Your Own

There's no one "correct" way to keep walking. There's only *your* way.

Now that you've built your foundation, you can continue however it suits your life:

- Keep your walk short and consistent

- Add variety with new routes or walking partners

- Walk with your dog, your playlist, your thoughts or your children

- Walk as meditation, exercise, creativity, or decompression

- Walk every day — or most days — or start again when life gets off track

This is your walking habit now. Shape it to fit your season of life. Let it grow with you. Let it support you in both the calm and the chaos.

Let Walking Become a Way of Being

When something becomes part of your lifestyle, it no longer needs force. It becomes natural — like making tea in the morning or brushing your teeth at night.

That's the goal here. Not to walk endlessly for its own sake, but to let walking become **woven into the fabric of your day**. A gentle structure. A grounding force. A gift to your body and mind.

You might not feel like walking every day. That's okay. But when you do, you'll know how. You'll remember why. And you'll return — because it feels like coming home.

You Don't Have to Walk Alone

Though walking can be beautifully solitary, you're not alone in this journey.

Millions of people — across countries, generations, and backgrounds — are discovering the power of this humble habit. Some walk for health. Some for healing. Some for peace. Some for joy.

And now, you're one of them.

If you want to stay connected or inspired:

- Join local walking groups
- Invite friends or family to join you once a week
- Follow walking or wellness communities online
- Track your journey in a journal or blog
- Share your story and encourage someone else to start

You never know who might be quietly waiting for permission to begin.

A Gentle Closing Thought

If you take nothing else from this book, take this:

You don't need to do everything to do something.

Some days, a long, energising walk will feel fantastic. Other days, five slow minutes will be all you can manage.

Both count.

This is not about perfection. It's about progress.
It's not about speed. It's about showing up.
It's not about the destination. It's about the direction.

And you, right now, are walking in the right direction.

Your Walking Life, From Here

So what now?

That's up to you.

Maybe you'll keep walking daily. Maybe you'll walk most days. Maybe you'll return to this book when you need a reset.

Whatever you choose, know this: walking is always available to you. No matter your mood, your weight, your job, your age, your level of fitness — the path is still there. Waiting. Ready.

And so are you.

So... put on your shoes.
Step outside (or don't — indoors counts too).
And take that next step.

You already know how.

Keep walking. Keep returning. Keep choosing yourself — one step at a time.

With warmth and encouragement,
Amelia Walsh

Also in the *Everyday Reset* series:

- *The Decluttering Reset*
- *The Gratitude Reset*
- *The Connection Reset*
- *The Habit Reset*
- (and now) *The Walking Reset*

How Walking Can Support Your Decluttering or Gratitude Practice

Walking may seem like a physical habit — a way to move your body and clear your mind — but it has a beautiful way of unlocking clarity and connection across other parts of your life. If you're working on decluttering or deepening a gratitude practice, walking can gently enhance both.

Walking supports decluttering by creating mental space. When we move, especially in quiet or natural surroundings, we give our minds room to breathe. Thoughts settle. Priorities rise to the surface. That cluttered cupboard or overstuffed drawer becomes less overwhelming — because walking reminds us we don't have to tackle everything at once. Just one thing. One drawer. One step. Often, ideas or decisions about what to let go of emerge naturally while we walk. We return home lighter — not just in body, but in intention.

Walking also nurtures gratitude. When we walk slowly, with awareness, we begin to notice the small things: light through the trees, the sound of birds, a neighbour's smile, the rhythm of our breath. Walking anchors us in the present moment — the very place where gratitude lives.

Each step becomes an invitation to say: *"I'm thankful for this moment. I'm thankful for this body. I'm thankful I get to move."* You don't have to force gratitude. Let it arise naturally, one step at a time.

So whether you're clearing your space or clearing your mind, remember: walking is a quiet companion to both. It doesn't demand much — just your presence. And it gives back in surprising, sustaining ways.

Printed in Dunstable, United Kingdom

70029104R00047